"WHAT DO YOU SEE?"

Copyright 1998

0

TABLE OF CONTENTS

SPECIAL THANKS TO THE FOLLOWING:

Uncle Jerry -St Clair

My Children—

William, Angela, and Toby Turner thank you so much for your unwavering support and encouragement throughout the writing of my vision. Your belief in me and my work has been invaluable. I couldn't have done it without you.

Thanks to my daughter-in-law Cindi for giving me the phone to get the pictures.

To Ciara, my amazing granddaughter, thank you so much for helping me make my dream come true."

Thanks to my assistant, Kellee Cullinane, for her guidance and help in using Microsoft Word to help me achieve my goals.

An AI generator created all the Pictures in this book. Microsoft AI generator

2

INTRODUCTION

Sarah's journey into the divine began with a dream, a gift from her uncle. As she ventured through celestial landscapes, guided by ethereal whispers, she discovered the universe's profound interconnectedness. From the birth of stars to the dance of galaxies, she saw a cosmic tapestry woven with love.

Ancient souls, their eyes filled with wisdom, imparted secrets of creation and the soul's eternal journey. Sarah's encounter with a celestial mirror revealed the multifaceted depths of her being. At that moment, she realized that the divine wisdom she looked for was not external but lived within.

The dream ignited a spiritual fire within her, transforming her life. She embraced the interconnectedness of all things, found peace in the cosmic dance, and discovered a profound connection to the divine. You are about to open the doorway to the subconscious mind, where laws of logic do not apply. Cross the bridge into a fragmented personality where the conscious divides and is separated from the world around us. Witness a journey through the supernatural, as the mysteries of fragmented consciousness come together in unity and individualization to form as one.

Experience the wonders beyond, taken in the mind's eye for memory, comes to life in true living color animation, and how of this; a new memory was obtained. The vision you are about to read occurs between these fragments of the human mind. The story's end leads to a bright future filled with wonderful surprises. A place where we can all experience amazing things forever.

TIME THEN -TIME AGAIN

Sarah felt lightness as if her

body was floating away. She was

looking down at herself, sleeping

peacefully on her bed. The room

seemed to glow with a soft,

golden light. It was as if watching

a dream within a dream. The clock

on the bedside table read. **1 AM**.

A gentle force drew her upward, towards something of the unknown. Fear mixed with excitement as she soared higher and higher. Then, a brilliant light filled her vision. A being of pure love and wisdom stood before her. It was as if she had come home. At that moment, Sarah knew everything. The universe unfolded before her with all its mysteries like a beautiful tapestry. She understood the interconnectedness of all living things, the reason for our existence, and the path to true peace. When she returned to her body, the world felt different. Ordinary things held extraordinary beauty. A simple flower became a masterpiece of creation. She felt a deep connection to everything around her. Driven by a quiet urge, Sarah began to write. Her words flowed effortlessly, like a gentle stream. She shared her experience, hoping to inspire others to look beyond the surface and discover the magic within themselves. People questioned her story, some with doubt, others with curiosity. But Sarah knew the truth resided in the heart. And so, she continued to share her journey, one word at a time, hoping to awaken the spirit of others. She was no longer a mere observer of life but a participant in a grand cosmic symphony.

Once a crushing burden, the weight of the world felt lighter, almost inconsequential. As Sarah hurtled towards the blue light, her consciousness expanded, encompassing lifetimes, galaxies, and the very fabric of existence.

She became aware of the interconnectedness of all things.

A vast cosmic tapestry; woven with threads of love, through light, and darkness. While in this expanded state, Sarah had seen it all. From the very beginning of life to the end of the world, she had watched everything. She saw animals evolve and civilizations rise and fall. She saw both good and bad things, happy and sad times. She saw hope and despair, the best and worst of humanity.

A profound sense of compassion washed over her. She understood the struggles of every living being, the challenges they faced, and the potential for growth and transformation that resided within each soul. Emerging from this cosmic journey, she found herself standing at the threshold of a new reality, a place where physical and spiritual realms converged. The blue light had transformed into a being of immense wisdom and compassion, its presence radiating love and acceptance. The chains of earthly existence were severed as if ascending into a realm beyond a veil. She was freed from the shadows of fear and the suffocating grip of mortality. Time didn't matter anymore, and she could see everything that ever happened in her life and everything that was about to come. A gentle voice guided her towards a bright blue light representing love and happiness. Although it was dark, Sarah felt calm and safe. She felt a strong connection to something bigger than herself, and it made her feel loved and at peace.

It was a love that everyone felt, a warmth that spread through their hearts, filling them with a newfound understanding. It was a love freely given, like a comforting hug that enveloped them in its embrace. This love was a gentle balm, soothing their souls and easing their worries. It was a beacon of hope, illuminating their path forward. It was a bond that connected them to something greater than themselves, a reminder that they were not alone, and we could share it with everyone in the world. A never-ending love that guides us and reminds us that we were never alone. Even in the darkness, her friends were with her, whispering encouragement. They traveled together, helping each other to move on from the past. The closer Sarah got to the light, the more she re-lived her past experiences, both happy and sad.

She understood that to be able to achieve happy memories, she had to let go of any sadness holding her back. No longer bound by a gravity of sorrow or the weight of human affliction, Sarah was lifted into a celestial embrace. The same force that shapes worlds and holds the soul captive was absent, leaving a void filled with an infinite, radiant love.

In this ethereal state, time unraveled its tapestry, revealing a panorama of existence untouched by the ravages of experience. Sarah traveled the long road of darkness through a giant telescope. "Confusion of time within time faded as Sarah drew nearer to the light."

With each step forward, Sarah was stepping into the past. Sometimes she even stepped backward, but then Sarah remembered something. Sometimes, painful memories can hold us back. However, it is possible to release the hurt and anger of yesterday. Some people dream of time travel, re-living cherished moments from the past. It's like replaying a favorite scene from a beloved book. But journeying into the future requires letting go of the past. Exciting possibilities await there. All negative thoughts and experiences associated with earthly life were permanently erased upon reaching the ethereal light. They were safely contained during the early part of the long, confined journey. As Sarah drew closer to the light, negativity dissipated, unable to withstand the prolonged exposure.

Consequently, any preconceived notions of evil became irrelevant. Darkness was eradicated shortly after beginning the journey. This explained the need for a group at the entry point. Their collective outpouring of love effectively silenced residual negativity and provided constant guidance. While traces of evil might have persisted, the ability to relive those traumatic experiences was eliminated. The visit was extraordinary. Sarah gained the ability to indefinitely pause time at any chosen moment, allowing for prolonged immersion in past experiences. She could revisit her entire life as if reading a book. Once a book is finished, there was no turning back. It was an incredible journey. The story's end leads to a bright future filled with wonderful surprises, a place where we can all experience amazing things forever. Before this, Sarah could only recall her family as blurry images in her mind's eye.

She now was experiencing their lives in vivid detail, with sound and movement. It was like a dream that felt completely real. Having these new memories is a special gift Sarah is grateful for, as she had no memories before. It's like she's been given a beautiful, colorful painting of her life to cherish. Sarah embarked on a journey through her past, pausing to relive cherished moments.

Once, she revisited her childhood, a time spent fishing with her brother, Eddie. They were inseparable, finding joy in each other's company. Every summer, they would wake up before dawn, their excitement palpable as they prepared for their fishing adventure. They would grab their poles, a bucket of worms they'd dug up the day before, and head out for an all-day adventure.

As they walked to the creek, the morning dew glistened on the grass, and the birdsong filled the air. The creek itself was a tranquil oasis, like crystal-clear waters flowing gently over the smooth rocks. They wandered to the bridge where they liked to fish.

They'd cast their lines into the cool depths, their hearts pounding with anticipation. Hours would pass as they chatted, laughed, and waited patiently for a nibble.

When they finally caught a fish, their excitement was boundless.

They would carefully remove the hook, admire their catch, and then release the smallest ones back into the creek. As the sun began to set, they would try to make it back home before the pole lights came on. Their arms were always heavy with a basket of freshly caught fish. They were so proud of their catch for the day. Sarah would also return to the creek with her mom and sister, Judy, where they would hunt for hellgrammites for hours.

With rolled-up pants, they searched for these creepy crawlies, which they sold to fishers to support their family.

Though the work was tough, the shared experiences strengthened their familial bond. Sarah loved experiencing her past life in vivid color.

She rediscovered the joy of swinging, playing with her dog, Rags, and even returning to school.

It was like living inside a beautiful painting. Every memory was a precious gift to cherish forever. Returning to her second-grade class was a delightful surprise. The first thing she did was search for her future husband, who was also a student there. Bill always claimed she had pushed him so hard on the swing that he'd almost reached the moon!

Though Sarah couldn't recall doing that, it was a humorous story. Sarah's heart swelled with a sense of belonging she'd never known. As she wandered deeper into this ethereal garden, she encountered beings of light, their forms shimmering with an iridescent glow. They communicated not with words but with feelings, a language of the soul that resonated within her.

A gentle breeze carried her through fields of endless green, where crystalline rivers flowed, their waters reflecting the sky's vibrant hues.

The animals she encountered were creatures of breathtaking beauty, their forms merging seamlessly with the lush landscape. As they danced around and played in the emerald fields, their joy was noticeable.

It was a world of pure harmony, where every living being existed in perfect balance.

As the sun began its descent, painting the sky in hues of orange and purple, Sarah found herself drawn to a colossal, ancient tree. Its roots seemed to delve deep into the very heart of the world, and its branches reached towards the heavens. As she approached, the tree seemed to hum with a life force of its own.

A sense of profound joy washed over Sarah as she recognized her beloved uncle. His presence was a comforting anchor in this unfamiliar yet enchanting realm. Together, they embarked on a journey through this new world, their laughter echoing through the crystalline air.

As they explored, they discovered hidden waterfalls cascading into shimmering pools, each one holding a unique energy. They danced among bioluminescent flowers, their light painting the night sky with celestial patterns. And they listened to the wisdom of the ancient trees, their roots delving deep into the heart of creation.

Yet, amidst this paradise, a subtle undercurrent of longing stirred within Sarah. She missed her loved ones, her friends, and the world she had left behind. She wondered if there was a way to bridge the gap between these two realms and share this extraordinary experience with those who would try to understand.

A bittersweet longing stirred within her. Oh, how she wished to see her uncle dance, to witness the joys she knew were trapped within his spirit. It felt like a dream, but it was so real. Sarah was looking right at him, but his face was different like it was not there.

And yet, she knew she was seeing a magnificent Angel, a real one. A warm feeling filled her soul as if she could feel his thoughts. Around them, everything was shining. Bright lights danced, and beautiful flowers covered the ground. It was like a magical garden, with apple trees that had the reddest, biggest apples ever seen.

The air was filled with music, unlike anything she had heard before. So clear and so beautiful. As she wandered through the enchanted garden, she noticed a peculiar glow emanating from a specific area.

Intrigued, she approached, her heart pounding with anticipation.

Before her there stood another colossal, crystalline tree unlike any she had seen before. Its leaves pulsed with an otherworldly light, and a soft hum filled the air.

Then her uncle spoke, not with words but with thoughts. He said, "You were born with a special light inside. It can grow brighter when you share kindness and love, but "Remember, your inner light can dim if you judge others. Be kind and loving to keep it shining bright."

Sarah had so many questions, but he answered them all before she could even ask. He said she was not supposed to be there yet. He could show her a little bit of heaven, but it was not time for her to stay. He told Sarah a few humans can stay for a while but must be pure and loving. If they are not, they cannot stay.

It was like a visit to a place of peace and wonder, a place where everything is perfect.

A long-forgotten memory surfaced like a treasure from the depths of her being. Voices echoed through time: "You're not supposed to be here!" A childish giggle followed, a sweet melody from a past that had been buried.

CELESTIAL REVERIE

Sarah was a child again, ten years old and hiding beneath her bed, her heart pounding with excitement. She had just sneaked into her house after returning from New York while living with her older sister, Judy.

Kathy found her peeking out from under the bed, her dark hair spilling onto the floor. Crawling out, Sarah emerged into a scene that felt both strange and comforting. Her sister, Kathy, once much shorter, stood before her, transformed into a big eleven-year-old. Kathy was a year older than Sarah, and her smile seemed to light up the room. Her hair, a cascade of golden curls, framed her face, always filled with joy. Her eyes—pools of blue—sparkled with a light that seemed to come from within. It was as if an angel had stepped into the room.

"You're home!" she screamed; her voice filled with delight. In that moment, all time stood still. It was as if the world outside had faded away, leaving only them. They hugged for the longest time.

"Oh, where is the baby?" Sarah asked, missing her baby sister, Lailonii, for nearly a year. A sense of peace washed over her. Holding her now two-year-old baby sister in her arms, Sarah felt a love so deep that it transcended the physical world.

Sarah's uncle's words echoed in her mind: "A child's light glows." It was as if he had seen into her soul, understanding the profound connection she felt.

In that instant, she knew she had experienced something sacred, a glimpse into a realm beyond our

ordinary world. Sharing secrets,
laughter, and a bond that time could
not break.

Then, a shift. The world exploded into a
kaleidoscope of colors. A gentle and
warm hand guided her into a realm of
pure light. Her uncle, a beacon in this
new reality, telepathically informed her
that he would be her guide throughout
this journey.

Sarah walked through a garden of emerald-green, protected by a soft, invisible shield. Time stood still, yet it moved with "true colors" and the brilliance of the souls as they moved with effortless grace. It was as if a veil had lifted. Suddenly lost in a world unknown yet deeply familiar, Sarah's heart pounded with excitement and wonder.

It was a reunion of souls, a reminder of the eternal love that binds us all. Sarah found herself in a place of pure magic. It was vast and open, filled with a soft, glowing light. Tiny, shimmering orbs floated around her, each one sending the world into a breathtaking masterpiece.

Every orb felt safe and protected, like a precious jewel in a hard solid case. They moved without a sound, but Sarah heard a beautiful melody. It was a place of perfect peace and harmony. She wanted to understand this magical world. Each little orb had its very own song and color, and they all blended in a glorious symphony.

Sarah floated among them, careful not to disturb their peace. Her uncle's voice brought her back to herself. "Close your eyes, Sarah, and find the deepest part of you," he said gently.

As she tried, she saw swirling colors and feelings. It was like looking into a sparkling ocean. Sometimes it was stormy, sometimes calm, but deep inside was a steady, warm light.

"That light, dear one," her uncle said, "is a piece of the universe within you. It's love."

The light swelled and brightened, engulfing everything in its radiant glow. Sarah felt a joy she'd never known before, pure and overwhelming. She was small, but part of something vast and wonderful.

When the light faded, she looked at her uncle, her eyes shining. "I saw a little bit of forever," she whispered.

He smiled. "And forever saw you, Sarah. It always has." Sarah felt a deep sense of peace. She knew she was connected to something much bigger than herself, and that was all that mattered.

Sarah felt like a sparkling star as she danced and played in the mirror's light, her movements graceful and joyful. She loved watching herself shimmer and shine. Softly, she called out to her uncle, careful not to disturb the tiny creatures around her.

She heard his whisper from the other side of the door, as clear as if he stood beside her. "You'll see the light," he promised, his voice as gentle as a summer breeze.

Then it happened. A blinding flash of light filled the room as if the universe itself had unveiled its hidden splendor. Sarah felt a sense of wonder and awe she'd never known. It was like a dream, yet more real than anything she'd ever experienced. A deep peace washed over her, and she felt a connection to something much bigger than herself.

A voice, deep and echoing like a canyon, filled the space. It felt like the voice was everywhere and nowhere at once. Sarah felt its power deep within her soul.

"The light of the body is the light of the eyes," her uncle said, his face calm and peaceful. She reached out to him, and suddenly, she was a little girl again. Sarah was two years old and perched precariously on a table when her mother burst into the room, her voice sharp.

"Get her out of that sugar bowl! Didn't you see her in there?" She scolded her sister; Judy then turned her attention to Sarah. "How many times do I have to tell you to stay out of the sugar bowl? I can't stand walking in sugar! Now stay out of it!"

"But I'm not in the sugar bowl," Sarah protested, sitting innocently on the table. "I don't fit."

"A child's light glows," her uncle's voice interjected, as if from a distant, wiser place.

Sarah stood still, bathed in a warmth that was both comforting and enlightening. It was as if a floodgate of understanding opened within her, and though a few words were spoken, Sarah grasped a profound truth. Sarah heard music.

It wasn't like any music she'd ever heard. It was like tiny bells ringing in the sky, a sweet song that seemed to come from far away. As she listened, colors swirled and danced in her mind, like a beautiful rainbow. She felt a sense of peace and joy wash over her as the music filled her soul. Her uncle smiled knowingly and said, "That's the music of your soul, Sarah. It's real and beautiful."

They closed their eyes and let the music wash them. It was peaceful and calming. Sarah felt a sense of wonder and peace she'd never known before.

Suddenly, a strong voice spoke in her heart. It was like a warm light filling her up. She knew it was God. And in that moment, she felt a deep connection to something much bigger than herself. Taking her uncle's hand, she felt a rush of love and understanding. It was as if they were floating on a cloud, surrounded by beauty and peace.

Sarah was practicing the piano. She was playing "The Little One Said" over and over. Her mom yelled, "I'm sick of hearing that same note! Play something else!" Sarah decided to play "Do You Hear What I Hear?" because it was Christmas. Sarah's brother, Pat walked into her playing the song when he asked.

"Why are you playing with your eyes closed?"

"I'm practicing 'I Can't Hear,'" Sarah replied.

He laughed and said, "You can't see what you're playing?"

"I can see!" she said.

"The boy with the glass eye can see, so I can too."

"That's stupid," Pat said. "Why are you practicing with your eyes closed?"

"Because I'm practicing 'I Can't Hear'! "Sarah shouted.

"You're crazy," he said, walking away.

"Can you please stop arguing?" Their mother asked as she entered the room. "Just let her practice."

THE OFFERING

Sarah's heart swelled with a mixture of love and concern as she recognized her siblings huddled together in the small, familiar space.

Their faces, usually alight with childhood innocence, were etched with a mixture of excitement and guilt. The once comforting sanctuary of their church now seemed to be charged with a secret tension.

Sarah understood their plight. Their family struggled, and a birthday gift for their mother was a distant dream. The temptation to divert a portion of the offering was a siren song, promising a glimmer of hope in their bleak reality. Sarah's uncle stood beside her; his presence brought a silent affirmation.

The divine message echoed through the room, a stark contrast to the children's carefully laid plans.

The words echoed through the sacred space, carrying the weight of ancient wisdom. "Give, and it will be given to you. Ask, and it shall be given."

A simple statement, yet profound in its implications. It was a message of abundance, not scarcity. It suggested a universe where generosity was the norm, not the exception. It spoke of a power greater than material possessions, a power that responded to the human spirit.

The children, caught in the grip of their limited perspective, could not yet grasp the fullness of these words. Their focus was on the immediate, tangible need—a gift for their mother. Yet, the divine message extended far beyond that, promising a harvest of blessings in response to their giving. As the children pondered their next move, the weight of the divine message began to settle on them.

It was a challenge to their assumptions, an invitation to a deeper level of faith and trust.   Sarah felt an overwhelming sensation of being filled yet empty simultaneously. It was as if her mind were a vessel, suddenly expanding to infinite capacity, yet still yearning to comprehend the vastness within.

Her uncle's words were like gentle rain, nourishing the newly tilled soil of her soul. He was a beacon, guiding her through the uncharted territory of her consciousness.

With each word, a new layer of understanding peeled away, revealing depths she never knew existed. A sense of peace washed over her, a profound tranquility that stemmed from a deep knowing.

She realized she was on the cusp of a great transformation, a journey into her heart.

"Mr. Piano Person," Sarah said, speaking to her piano. "Are you lonesome tonight? Do you want me to play some beautiful music for you? Oh, how I wish I could get that music out of you. I know you have beautiful music inside of you. I just don't know how to get it out." Sarah said, while gently touching the piano keys. "I'm going to stay with you forever, so you can teach me all the music you have inside of you. Please play some of your music for me. I promise I'll practice what you teach me. I promise! Please?" Sarah begged her beloved piano player. I just love you so much. If you teach me, I will never forget. Please?"

If you teach me, I will never forget. Please?"

Sarah felt a surge of energy as her uncle's hands touched her eyes. It was as if a cosmic light was being ignited within her, spreading warmth and understanding through every fiber of her being. Love, pure and unconditional, enveloped her, expanding outward to fill the entire room with a serene glow.

Suddenly Sarah felt a shift in the universe. She opened her eyes to see her uncle had materialized before her, a tangible presence with a touch of ethereal beauty. His hair was streaked with silver. His gentle face held a wisdom of ages. In his hands, he held a photograph of a baby, its eyes mirroring the depths of the universe.

A profound connection pulsed through Sarah. She recognized the baby as a piece of herself, a soul yet to bloom. The image vanished as quickly as it appeared, replaced by the sight of her uncle standing beside a luminous, cloud-like form. It was a being of pure energy, surrounded by a protective aura of color. A sense of awe filled

Sarah. She was witnessing the birth and growth of a soul, a glimpse into the eternal tapestry of life. Her understanding of the universe expanded exponentially, and with it, a profound sense of peace and purpose. "The unity you feel is in the truth. The truth is in the tree of life. A child's light glows."

The voice continued to guide Sarah, each word a gentle push forward on her journey of self-discovery. As she watched her younger self struggle and learn, profound empathy washed over her. She understood the challenges of childhood with a clarity she'd never experienced before.

The room around her began to change. The familiar surroundings of her childhood home emerged, filled with the warmth of family and the innocence of youth. It was as if she were reliving her life, moment by moment, but with a detached perspective.

A sense of wonder and gratitude filled her heart. She saw the love and support that had shaped her into the person she is today. The challenges, the triumphs, and the lessons learned were all part of a beautiful tapestry of life.

As she continued to journey through her past, she realized that each experience, no matter how small or insignificant it may have seemed, had contributed to her growth and evolution.

Sarah stood in awe; her senses overwhelmed by the intensity of the experience. The world had been reborn in a blaze of light and sound, and she was at its center.

Another shift in time had Sarah back in her childhood home again.

Seven-year-old Sarah sat at the piano, her fingers dancing across the keys. Her father accompanied her on the mandolin while her older brother Bobby blared his trombone from his room upstairs. Across the hall, Dixie tootled on her trumpet. In the kitchen,

Judy and Ted banged out a rhythm on the table with drumsticks.

Sarah's little brothers Toby and Eddie ran into the house from the backyard and called out for Sarah to come.

Sarah jumped down from the piano bench and excitedly ran to the boys.

"Where are you all going?" Sarah's dad calls out. "Come on, follow me," the boys yell as they run back out the door, letting the screen door slam behind them.

Look, I found something in the yard. Her brother Eddie whispers. Eddie shows her an old arrowhead he found while digging in the dirt. "This has to be worth lots of money," he said. Don't tell anyone but I'm gonna' hide it in the wall to keep it safe.

Like a symphony, the sounds of music - cherished memories. Sarah had long forgotten until she returned to see her home again.

The music filled her with joy and recollection, bringing the past vividly back to life. In her mind's eye, Sarah took a mental snapshot of this beautiful moment, a treasure to cherish forever.

The voice, a whisper of cosmic wisdom, had ignited a spark within her. With newfound clarity, she looked at her uncle. His eyes held a depth of understanding that was both comforting and inspiring.

She realized she was no longer a passive observer but an active participant in this extraordinary journey.

THE LIGHT WITHIN

A sense of purpose filled her. She was ready to embrace the light and walk the path that lay ahead. The darkness that had once clouded her vision was now a distant memory, replaced by a radiant hope.

Dazzled by the vibrant display, Sarah shielded her eyes with her arms. The music reached a deafening peak as colors whirled around her.

Then, a deep, soothing voice filled her mind.

"Walk while you have the light. Darkness will be your guide no more." The world was transformed. Not only could she see, but she understood. A newfound clarity washed over her, like a cool rain on a scorching day.

Sarah took one step forward and drifted one step back. One step forward again, and Sarah was at the front door of her house. She knocks.

"Who is it?" Sarah's mother called.

"It's me," Sarah called back.

"Who's me?"

She yells again. "It's just me." Sarah says again, "It's just me." Sarah took a step forward and she found herself knocking on another door.

"Who's there?" Sarah's sister called out.

"It's me," Sarah said to her.

"Who's me?" her sister asked. She took a second step forward and Sarah was running to show her Daddy her dolly.

"Daddy, Daddy look! Do ya know who this is?" Sarah asks as she holds up her dolly.

"No," her daddy says, "who is it?" She took one step forward and saw her little brother.

"Do you know who I am?" Sarah asks her brother.

"Yeah, you're my sister, who do you think you are? Here this is for you." Her brother Toby says, as he hands her a little star that had fallen off of his school paper.

Sarah's mind was a whirlwind of sensations. The familiar echoes of childhood questions mingled with the celestial symphony that surrounded her. Every step was a leap into the unknown, guided by an unseen hand.

Sarah was again at another place in time, where she could see a busload of siblings filling a bus for Sunday school. Easter Sunday was the only day the children truly looked forward to going to church.

Sarah's mother would sew her and her sisters the most beautiful Easter dresses. She would piece together scraps from her sisters' hand-me-downs, transforming them into works of art. It was a labor of love, a testament to her creativity and the joy she found in crafting something special for her children.

Laying the fabric on the floor, she never needed a pattern. Her skilled hands guided the scissors with precision cuts. Each stitch was a testament to her love and dedication. The dresses, though made from humble materials, were masterpieces, symbols of her unwavering love for her children.

The girls loved wearing their dresses to Sunday school.

As Sarah stood on the cliff of this extraordinary experience, she felt a strange connection to all that was.

She felt like she was part of something amazing. "The colors, the music, the love—they're all like pieces of a big puzzle, slowly coming together to make a beautiful tapestry woven in the mine eye.

Sarah relives moment by moment of past events.

Sarah is four years old. Her sister, Judy, is thirteen and teaching her how to play hopscotch.

"First you put one foot down, then you jump! Then both feet, jump! One foot, then jump!"

Judy hops slowly so Sarah can watch. "Now it's your turn."

Sarah tries as she sings; "ya take one step, now ya take one step; and take one step."

Sarah hears her sister giggle.

"It's okay!" Judy giggles. "You'll understand one day, you'll just have to practice."

The words "Come to me, and I will show thee!" echoed in her mind, a promise of further revelation. The pathway of colors, a bridge to the divine, stretched out before her. With her uncle's firm grip and the unwavering support of the celestial choir, she took the first step. As Sarah took another step forward, her uncle slowly glided in front of her.

He held both hands high in the air. She looked up, and high in the sky was a great, glorious white angel.

The lights that emanated from him were like that of a gleaming sun.

She could feel the radiance and warmth of the rays as they enveloped her in a blanket of security. Musical voices were singing, and distinct horns were sounding. Instantly, as if given a direct order, everything came together, creating a magnificent symphony composed of the greatest of perfection. The lights stopped flashing, and the colors, as if following a cosmic command, arranged themselves into a flawless rainbow. Sarah extended her hands toward the colors and music and felt an overwhelming surge of pure, undivided love.

"Tiny chimes, blessed by the moment, sang their silent song, while an angelic voice whispered a melody of praise." Though he sang gently, it was perceived as superior. The voice harmonized with the little chimes, singing unto the Lord in perfect harmony. The words that were sung were, "Come to me, and I will show you!" Sarah's uncle gripped her hand firmly, and a glorious rainbow twinkled light, filling her with wonder.

Sarah's eyes captured the moment, a precious memory etched deep within her soul. The colors were phenomenal, staying in perfect order, side by side, obeying a law, a force of togetherness. One color held to the next color, and the next, and so on, forming a perfect roadway leading up into the heavens. Walking along this pathway made from the colors of a rainbow is something Sarah knew she would never forget.

Sarah saw all the colors of the rainbow in the path, but the ground was covered in a soft, green carpet, like the grass she played on as a child. Tiny bits of rainbow light fell on Sarah's head like soft, sparkling rain.

The ground was a breathtaking mosaic of colors, a swirling tapestry of green, red, blue, and yellow. Yet, no matter how close they came, the colors never blended. They remained distinct, each with their own vibrant identity. It was as if an invisible force kept them apart, a magical puzzle where the pieces fit perfectly without merging. The ground sparkled like a bed of precious gems, each color shining with its own unique light.

The angel was still singing a sweet, peaceful song. Their voices, like a gentle breeze, caressed her heart. She could feel their song weaving through the threads of her past, present, and future.

"When you look out the window, what do you see, where do you go?"

"I don't know," Sarah answered back. "I go to school. I remember sitting at my desk, and then it's time to go home." Sarah was thirteen years old.

Sarah stared out the window, her gaze lost in the gray expanse. The rain splattered against the glass, creating an endless, rhythmic pattern. Beyond the blurred panes, the world was a muted canvas of gray buildings and hurrying people. A deep sigh escaped her lips.

"I see a rainbow that shines bright with light."

"And where is this rainbow?" Her teacher asked, looking out the window.

"It's in the morning star."

"What do you see, where do you go?" Sarah's doctor asked, his voice gentle but firm. Sarah, once lost in the gray expanse, now met his gaze. Her voice was small.

"I... I don't know," she stuttered. The words felt foreign on her tongue. "I see the rain. I go to school."

The doctor's eyebrows raised slightly. "And when you're not at school?"

Sarah hesitated. "Home. My room. Sometimes I look out the window." A long pause.

The doctor nodded slowly. "And what do you see then?"

Sarah's eyes drifted back to the window as if searching for an answer.

"Nothing much. Just the sky. Or the trees." But mostly, she could see the morning star. Sarah's voice was soft, almost a whisper. Her eyes held a distant look. The doctor's hand tightened slightly on her arm.

"The morning star, you say?" He tried to sound calm, but his voice trembled slightly. "Sarah, do you understand that the morning star is a planet, not a star?"

Sarah's eyes remained fixed at a point in the distance. "It's different," she murmured. "It's special."

SEVEN ANGELS

An angel appeared directly in front of
Sarah. Suddenly, one angel became
seven.

They were shining, beautiful beings,
glowing like pure pearls. Like a rainbow,
a colorful path stretched out in front of
them. The angels had a golden circle
around their heads, like a halo, and
held a bright golden stick. The gold and
the angel's light seemed to be one.

The golden circles danced around them as they moved closer like playful spirits. The colors sparkled with every step they took. "What do you see?" Her Uncle asked. "Angels," Sarah replies.

Seven angels stood nearby, watching, as a soft, heavenly song filled the air. The melody she heard was as gentle as a breeze, but still sending the most powerful touching message to her soul in a way she had never felt before. The melody she heard was...

"When you wish upon a star, it makes no difference who you are, -- Anything your heart desires-- Will come to you."

The words Sarah heard being sung to the same melody were...

*When you wish upon a dream, a hope,
a wish, a golden gleam. The heart's
desire, a shining star, a wish fulfilled,
not distant far.*

*A twinkling hope, a magic sight, A
dream come true, a pure delight."*

Suddenly, the angel in the middle
spoke. His voice was like a strong wind.

No words came out, but Sarah felt
alive and new inside as she could
understand his silent words. It was like
fresh air filled her whole being like she
was born again. Every tiny part of her
had a new way of seeing as if her eyes
could look everywhere at once.
Suddenly, the candlesticks vanished

from the angels' hands. The angel in the middle held up seven sparkly stars.

Sarah couldn't believe her eyes when the stars changed into seven strong white horses, and on each horse sat seven more shining angels. Each of the new angels wore a shiny metal headpiece and a chest cover that looked like brass armor. They seemed ready to fight at any moment.

She could feel their power, how fast they were, and how ready they were to protect her. She felt completely calm as the angels started to speak. The moment the angels spoke, Sarah felt overwhelmed.

She fell to the ground and cried out, "I know you! I know you!" with a strong loud voice that she couldn't believe was her own. Beautiful ringing sounds filled the air as each angel rode past. The Lord held her steady, and she felt strong and wise. She knew with certainty that He was all-powerful. One by one the Angels spoke to Sarah as they galloped past:

"In the hush of the night, a plea sounded, when I answered you; You called me Jessica.

A silent plea echoed when I answered you, Sarah, you called me Jennifer.

Even in the darkest hour, I was there for you, I pulled you from despair. You called me Johnny.

The moment you cried out in the darkness, I was there. You called me

Tabitha.

And when the thief returned, I answered your call once more Sarah, you called me Sabrina. Though your vision was obscured, your spirit shone, Sarah. I answered, a guiding light in the darkness. You called me Samantha. Through the confusion of time, your voice reached me, Sarah. I was ever-present. And when the thief returned, I was there again, answering your call. You called me Dorthy."

Every one of these angels she knew. She knew them then, and she knew them now. Like a thunderclap, they spoke, together.

"We were there, and we are here. You couldn't see and you couldn't tell. We were there and we are here. You can see and you can tell. We are now and we are one."

A blinding flash happened as if there was a surge of power, and the angels were gone. A symphony of tiny bells, like musical gifts from the heavens, surrounded Sarah. The angels' singing was still the most wonderful music, and the lights shone together in perfect beauty. High in the sky, seven bright stars appeared. Sarah watched as the stars joined together, pulled by a strong, loving force, becoming one brilliant morning star.

It shimmered and sparkled and was the brightest star in the sky. Sarah felt peace and beauty, and deep inside the mind's eye, Sarah took a picture. Then there was silence, as though she was stepping through a time portal. Sarah was visiting a long-forgotten memory.

"Come up here! I wanna show you something!" Sarah's father calls. "Hurry!" Sarah was six years old. She was stooping on the grass in her backyard. In her hand, she had a bag of clovers.

She'd been looking for four-leaf clovers
all morning.

The grass was still wet from the rain,
and in the sky was a beautiful rainbow.
"Hurry up!" Her father repeats.

"What do you have? Do you have
something for me?!" Sarah asked
excitedly as she ran to him. "Yeah, I
have something for you!" He grabs her
little hand, and they ran to the side of

the house, and right there lying on the ground were two baby birds.

"Oh, my goodness!" Sarah giggled gleefully.

"Do you want to take care of them?" Her father asks. "Oh, my goodness!" She giggles again, "I love them so much, I'll take very good care of them. You'll see, I promise I will." Sarah says.

Her father gave her a little box. "If you feed them every day, they will get fur. Then they will grow feathers on their wings and fly. But you gotta' feed them every day, and you can never forget." he says to Sarah, as he gently places the tiny birds in the box.

"Oh no! I will never forget."

Sarah took a single step and was met with a magnificent, angelic voice filling the air like a trumpet's call. It was her mother, singing a sacred hymn. Her voice carried the words, "On-a-hill-far-away," each syllable a masterpiece of melody. The most dazzling lights shimmered and danced as she sang, casting a divine glow upon the scene.

Sarah took another step and heard her father's voice, "C'mon up here, I wanna show ya!" He urged her to hurry, "We're going to have a storm!" Sarah giggled as she ran towards him, "Do you have something for me?"

"Yeah! I have something for you." Her father replies.

"Again!? You have something for me again!?" asks Sarah,

with excitement and curiosity in her tiny voice. He grabs her little hand, and they run to the side of the house, and right there on the ground are two more baby birds.

"Oh, my goodness!" Sarah giggled gleefully.

"And you can never forget." Her father says. "Oh no! I can never forget." Sarah replies.

Sarah took one step and hears an angel calling her name.

"C'mon over here, I wanna show ya'." Sarah looks up and sees her mother.

Sarah hears the thunder; it sounds far away. The sky is dark from the storms.

"Do you have something for me?" Sarah asks in wonderment.

"Yes, I have something for you." Sarah's mother holds in her hands an eyedropper. "This is what you'll use to feed your baby birds. Don't forget." She spoke.

Sarah surrendered to the embrace of stillness. Her body, weary from its earthly journey, longed for the sanctuary of slumber.

A gentle warmth enveloped her, like a loving hand guiding her into a profound peace. She drifted, weightless and carefree as if cradled on the softest clouds. In this tranquil space, awareness expanded.

A luminous light filled her vision, yet she resisted its pull, basking in the depths of relaxation.

Time ceased to exist as she merged with the infinite. A whisper of curiosity arose, a gentle nudge toward waking.

But the allure of this ethereal realm was too strong. She yielded once more, allowing the universe to cradle her in eternal rest.

THIRSTY

Sarah was startled by her uncle's voice.

"Sarah, come with me."

She found herself in what seemed like a desert. The sun was beating down on Sarah, relentlessly beating against her exposed skin. Grains of sand clung to her sweat-dampened face, a gritty mask of the desert's embrace.

Beside her, little Toby stumbled, his small hand gripping hers tightly. Their journey seemed endless, a path stretching into eternity. Thirst gnawed at Sarah's insides, a relentless predator. Her throat burned a fiery furnace.

She glanced at Toby; his small frame etched with exhaustion. His eyes, usually sparkling with mischief, were now dull with fatigue. A sob choked in her throat, but no tears fell.

With a final, desperate effort, Sarah pushed on. The world seemed to tilt and sway. Just when she thought she couldn't endure another step, Toby's voice, small but determined, broke through the haze.

"We're almost there, Sarah," he said, his voice filled with courage that belied his age. Hope, a fragile flame, flickered to life within her.

She looked at Toby, his face a mask of determination. In that moment, she saw not just her little brother, but a symbol of resilience, a testament to the human spirit.

As they stumbled upon a small oasis, a woman's outstretched hand offered salvation. Cool water quenched their thirst, and Sarah felt a wave of gratitude wash over her. She looked at Toby, his small hands empty, his face serene. He had found a strength within himself that amazed her.

In the heart of the desert, Sarah had discovered an inner wellspring of courage and resilience. The journey had been arduous, but the rewards were immeasurable. Beside her, her little brother stood as a living testament to the power of the human spirit.

Closing the door behind her, Sarah was able to regain a memory long forgotten. Stepping further along, directly to the front of her appeared another door. Sarah's uncle reached out, opened the door, and they both entered a room.

SECRET THING

The walls were created from the heavens, and Sarah had the delicate feeling of floating. She saw beautiful designs of the richest pastel blue,

green, pink, and yellow as they blended slightly to form a glimmer of essence on the walls.

Sarah heard a slight humming sound, a barely audible hum surrounding the room. "What is that sound?" Sarah whispered to her uncle. "Why am I whispering?" she whispered again. "This is a special place, and this is a secret thing!" Sarah's uncle said, looking directly at her. With his look, she was filled with the spirit of understanding.

"A special place. A secret thing." Over and over, it repeated in her mind until Sarah was at another place long passed.

To a place where yesterday never was, today never is, and tomorrow never comes. A place that had been stored away, never to reopen, or so she thought. Sarah was six years old. Her grandma handed her an album.

"Here, this is for you. This is a special album. Please don't break it. Put it in a special place somewhere so it won't get broken, and when you get mad, don't break it, okay?" The album had a Christmas picture on the cover. Baby Jesus was lying in a cradle.

"Oh, thanks, Grandma, I will take very good care of it, I promise," Sarah said as she ran to put it in a special place.

Memories started flooding back one after another. Sarah was five years old. "Oh, I'm five years old today!" Sarah shouted as she jumped out of bed. Her mean sister is seven. She sang a secret, and Sarah didn't like her singing a secret to her.

"I know what you're getting for your birthday, and you don't know!" she sang.

"What is it?" Sarah asked. "It's a secret, and I can't tell you." She sang.

"You better tell me!" Sarah shouted as she ran downstairs, yelling to her mommy. "Mommy!" she yelled. "I hate her, she said she knows what I'm getting for my birthday, and she won't tell me!"

"It's a secret thing," her mother said. "You're not supposed to tell a secret." "Oh?" Sarah replied. "When will I be getting it?" As another door opened Sarah saw herself as a small child.

Sarah was two years old. She was
standing in the hallway just outside the
kitchen. She saw her mother standing
by the stove. Sarah took her baby
brother's bottle. She sneaked to the
back door with it and her older brother,
Ted, saw her.

"What do you got in your hands?" He
whispered. Sarah tried to hide the
bottle so he couldn't see it and he said,
"Put that bottle back right now!" She
puts the bottle in her mouth and her
brother says again, "Listen to me!
Mom's got eyes in the back of her head,
she'll see ya with that bottle, you better
give it back!"

Sarah sucks on the bottle and she hears
her mother yell, "You put that bottle

back right now unless you want a whipping!"

"I told you she'd hear ya." Her brother says.

"Daddy! Watch me! Can you see me?" Three-year-old Sarah hung upside down from the big tree in her yard. Her little legs were wrapped tight around a strong branch.

"I see you, sweetie!" her dad replied, smiling.

But her mom screamed, "Get her down from there! She'll hurt herself!" She rushed over to help her down. "Don't do that again!" Her mom scolded her, her voice shaking. "You scared me half to death!"

"But it was fun!" Sarah giggled.

"I know, honey, but it's dangerous. Let's go inside and draw some pictures."
Sarah happily ran inside and sat at the kitchen table.

Sarah was drawing a picture of a house, but it didn't look like a house.

"Draw your house like this," Sarah's mother said, and she draws a big, beautiful house for her.

"Oh, I can do that, watch me!" Her older sister is watching her draw the house. "Are you still watching me?" Sarah asked her sister, Judy.

"Yes, I'm watching you," she says.
When Sarah was finished, Judy said,

"This is great! Mom, look at the house she drew, isn't she smart."

"Yup," her mother says, "she's very bright!" Sarah ran outside to show her daddy. "Daddy! Daddy! Look at my house I drew. Mom says I'm very bright. Am I bright?" She asked her daddy.

"Yeah, you're so bright, you just glow in the dark." Her daddy says to her.

Holding her uncle's hand, Sarah found herself in a place of wonder. The sky was perfect, clear blue, like a sparkling jewel. A small cloud hovered still, right in front of her. Suddenly, the world was filled with a golden light – a rich, vibrant amber. It felt like this light could seep into every part of her, filling her with a longing she couldn't explain. It was as if her soul was reaching out for something it desperately needed.

Then, her uncle stepped out of the golden light. He looked amazing, but words couldn't describe what she saw. A powerful energy surrounded him, an energy she had never felt before. It was like a new life was flowing into her, changing her from the inside out. A whirlwind of golden light swirled and danced around them, a mesmerizing spectacle of color and movement. Each hue, from the softest yellow to the brightest gold, seemed to shimmer and pulsate with life. As their eyes adjusted to the dazzling display, a figure emerged from the heart of the light.

Cloaked in a radiant glow, the figure moved towards them with serene grace, its form as pure and ethereal as freshly fallen snow.

A gentle rain began to fall, and Sarah and her uncle were bathed in a brilliant white light, feeling cleansed and renewed, like newborn spirits. Sarah stood there, awestruck and filled with peace she had never known. The light was breathtaking. Brighter and more dazzling than anything she has ever seen. As he took a step, tiny white crystals fell from him like crystalline rain, gently covering her. When he stood beside her, a powerful love exploded within her. Unlike anything she had ever known. He looked directly into her eyes and his energy intensified as his hand touched her shoulder. A powerful force erupted like a mighty wind, and she was overwhelmed. "Sarah can't describe what she felt.

He placed his hand on a small cloud-like form and spoke in a loud, unfamiliar language. Thousands of tiny cloud beings from afar joined in, all speaking the same unknown tongue. Their voices combined into a rushing wind, carrying the mighty waters. The sound grew louder and closer, surrounding her.

She couldn't understand the words, and she couldn't speak. Her soul connected with this power and love and felt a perfect union, complete and whole. Never had she felt such a powerful, spiritual connection. No love on Earth could compare to this. She wanted to stay in this moment forever, experiencing a love only possible through God's grace. "Where are all those voices coming from? What is everyone saying?" Sarah asked her uncle, filled with wonder as she tried to understand what she was hearing.

"We understand in part and see in part," he replied.

"And through the seed, all the world will be blessed. The love you feel is found in truth. Truth is found in the tree of life. You will feel many things as you see. Listen with your heart, you will understand."

She listened closely, and she understood. Sarah knew what she heard, and she could speak! Sarah told her uncle what she was hearing, exactly as it was being said.

"All people will come together in truth. You are part of a new generation, and you will see. Now is the right time, and everyone will see. Those who believe will believe. Those who don't believe will believe. And again, those who believe will believe."

Brilliant lights flooded the room with stunning colors, then there was silence. Sarah couldn't comprehend what she was hearing while her eyes intently focused on the small, cloud-like shape. She tried to discern what lay hidden within. It was like looking through a thick, protective glass barrier. Finally, Sarah saw something.

It wasn't her mother she saw, it was her sister, and she was cradling a small baby.

"How did my sister get in there with that baby?" Sarah asked her uncle. "Who is that?" she asked again. Sarah could hear a lullaby being sung. She knew the voice. It was the voice of her mother. Somehow her sister was singing, but the voice she heard was her mother's, and she sang:

"Amazing grace, how sweet the sound, that saved a wretch like me. I once was lost, but now am found, was blind, but now I see." "You called him Jamie," her uncle said.

"I don't know that baby. Whose baby is that? Is it my sister, Judy's baby? I saw a picture of a baby that looks like this one." Sarah said.

"Your sister's baby died when he was six months old." "How can my sister be with her baby now if he died so many years ago, and my sister is still alive?"

"This is the time, Holy Spirit. This is the right time."

Her uncle spoke as the singing continued.

"T'was grace that taught my heart to fear, how precious did that grace appear, the hour I first believed. Thousands of voices were singing with her mother and sister. Each voice was unfamiliar, yet she heard them differently. She felt the sound of tiny bells, like perfect harmony, a masterpiece created only by God's hands forever.

"Through many dangers, toils, and snares, I have already come. T'was grace has brought me safe thus far, and grace will lead me home."

Sarah was quiet and didn't know what was happening. She thought about a place where today was now, tomorrow was a dream, and yesterday didn't exist. A place where she hadn't seen anything yet.

Sarah was sitting at her desk. She looked at her school papers. She covered her ears and couldn't see. Her teacher was next to her and said, "Look! You got all the answers right!"

Sarah said, "L-O-O-K. Does that mean I got everything right?"

Her teacher said, "Yes! You got everything right. Can you see the eyes on the word 'l-o-o-k'?"

Sarah said, "I don't know. Can I?"

Her teacher said, "I don't know. Can you?"

Sarah said, "I don't know. Can I try?"

Her teacher said, "Come with me. I will show you something. These are your spelling words. When I looked at your paper, I saw you were thinking about other things. Look, do you see it?"

Sarah said, "Oh, yeah, I see it!"

Her teacher said, "Do you know what 'emit' means?"

Sarah said, "No, I don't know that word."

Her teacher said, "I know. But I saw 'emit' on your paper and 'time' on mine. That's why I tried something. I looked at your paper in the mirror and saw 'time'. You see things like looking in a mirror. Do you understand?"

Sarah said, "I think so. My head is screwed on backward. That's what my brother, Pat, said. Kids think I am weird. Is that right?"

Her teacher said, "No, no, no. You are special. Sometimes it's hard to know what you mean. When someone says something, you don't understand, ask them. Don't just think about it by yourself."

Sarah said, "Oh okay!"

Her teacher said, "Good. Take these papers home and show them to your mom. Write your letters like you read a book."

Sarah said, "Oh no! I can't find my papers! I lost them!"

Her mom said, "What's wrong?"

"I lost my school papers; I was going to show you. The teacher drew eyes on it. I can't find it!"

Her mom said, "What does it look like?"

Sarah said, "It has big eyes. I got all the answers right. The teacher drew eyes so I could see it. Mom, do you understand me?"

Her brother, Ted, said, "I think you came from Mars."

Sarah said, "I didn't come from Mars. The stork brought me."

Ted said, "The stork dropped you at the wrong house or on your head."

Her mom said, "Stop it! No more talking like that."

Sarah said, "Did the stork drop me at the wrong house?"

Then her other brother Pat said, "There is no stork."

Sarah said, "Yes there is! Did he? Mom?"

"What did you say your school papers looked like?"

Her mother asked again.

  Sarah heard a voice. The voice had the power to penetrate her soul yet was as gentle as a feather floating silently. The voice has power in each word, embedding enormous amounts of information into every tiny particle of Sarah's ever existence.

"All bodies are not the same bodies." The voice said, and like silently drifting in the wind, she traveled, she traveled to another place, to another time, to a place of ...

Sarah was sitting at her desk. "Class," The teacher says, "did you all bring your ears today?".

"I did, I did!" Sarah says excitedly as she holds her earmuffs high in the air.

"Yes!" Everyone giggles. Sarah turned to see all the other earmuffs but there were none, she quickly put the earmuffs back into her desk when the teacher said.

"OK Class. Zip your mouth and open your ears. We have been practicing all week for today, and I was hoping you could listen very closely to what I have to say. You will only fill in one space for each question. If you don't know the answer, continue with the next question. You can only write on this test with this special pencil. When you think you are finished, go back, and fill in the ones you missed. I trust that everybody understands what to do. If you do not understand you should ask me now."

Her teacher continued, "When everyone is finished with this test, I have, in the box by my desk, a beautiful red apple' for each one of you. OK class, are you ready? One, two, three...Go!"

Sarah was surrounded by a bright shining light. Standing in front of her was her uncle, but he looked different, like a shining person.

Sarah's uncle whispered secrets into her ear, secrets of a world beyond her sight. He told her she was chosen, a vessel for the unseen.

She could peer through the veil of time and witness the tapestry of events yet to unfold. If she could conquer the trials that lay ahead, a prize awaited her: the Tree of Life, a beacon of eternal wisdom and power. But Sarah was not alone in this quest. Her uncle revealed that a celestial light would soon illuminate the hearts of all whiles granting them the gift of vision.

He urged Sarah to be a guiding star, a beacon of hope in the darkness. For in her purity and kindness lay the key to unlocking the magic that awaited the world. Then, colorful lights started to dance around, and beautiful music filled the air. Sarah's uncle was singing a special song.

Suddenly, Sarah found herself surrounded by countless people, each glowing like a star. They were filled with joy and cheer, their laughter infectious. A vibrant rainbow arched across the sky, and warm, cleansing rain began to fall. Sarah felt weightless as if she were floating on air.

Then, without warning, she plummeted downward, landing in a new and unfamiliar place. It was like a dream. Sarah's uncle appeared beside her, saying, "I'll show you everything.

A CHILD'S PERSPECTIVE

Little Sarah, a mere four years old,
scrunched her nose in disgust at the
foul odor of the tar pack on her chest.
"Mommy, it smells yucky," she whined.
Her gaze then fell upon her little
brother, Randy. "He smells yucky too!"
she declared. Her mother approached
them, a look of concern etched on her

face. "I know it doesn't smell good," she explained, "but it's to keep you safe. You have to wear it." "How much longer?" Sarah's little brother Randy asked, his voice muffled by the smelly pack.

"You'll wear it until…"

Their mother paused, her eyes meeting their father as he entered the room, a look of sympathy on his face.

"But Mom, Sarah said, yesterday you said…"

"Forget yesterday," her mother interrupted, her tone firm.

Sarah persisted. "Daddy, Mom said yesterday we could take this off tomorrow, and it's tomorrow."

"Would you just forget yesterday!" her mother exclaimed, her voice rising. "It's not tomorrow, it's today," her father corrected gently. "Tomorrow never comes. It's always today."

He placed a hat on Sarah's head. "I know this stuff smells bad, but you have to wear it to get better. Will you do this for me?

Believe me, you'll only wear it until"... He turned to the mother with a hopeful look in his eyes. "Tomorrow? Maybe."

Sarah's eyes widened. "Tomorrow, tomorrow... But tomorrow never comes..."

"Will you do these things for me? Will you do these things for me? Believe in the power..."

A soft glow began to emanate from the tar pack, casting strange, dancing shadows on the walls. Sarah's heart pounded with excitement. She reached out to touch the pack, but her hand was met with a warm, comforting sensation. Suddenly, she felt a gentle tug on her hand. She looked down and saw a tiny, glowing figure standing beside her bed. It was a figure made of light, with sparkling eyes and a gentle smile.

"I'm here to help you," the figure said. "I'm the guardian of tomorrow."

Sarah's eyes widened in wonder. "What is tomorrow like?" she thought. "It's a place of hope and healing; A place where you'll be free from pain and sickness."

Sarah's heart filled with joy.

"Can I go there?" she asked in her heart eagerly awaiting a reply.

Jesus's presence fills the room, and they drift off to sleep.

Sarah was 3 years old, her heart pounded in her chest as she clutched her beloved doll.

"Mommy! Mommy! Look at my dolly!" she cried, tears streaming down her face.

The once-perfect doll lay with a broken arm at her feet. "She's broken," Sarah wailed, cradling the doll without an arm attached, in her hands. "Can you fix her?"

Her mother knelt beside her, examining the damage. "What happened to her arm?"

"Tony the pony stepped on it and broke it off," Sarah sobbed.

Her older brother, Bobby held up the broken limb.

"I know what to do," Sarah's other sister, Kathy chirped. "There's an old doll in the attic with no legs. I'll get it for you, you can use her arm.

Sarah's eyes lit up with hope. "When will she be fixed?" she asked her mother eagerly.

"In a little while," her mother reassured her. "Now go play, and she'll be all better soon."

Sarah nodded; her doll clutched tightly to her chest. As she ran out the door, a chilling whisper seemed to echo in her mind: ***In a little while, you won't see me. Then you will see me.***

Hours later, Sarah sat on the couch, gently combing her doll's hair.

"Hey," her sister Penny called out. "I thought the pony stepped on your dolly."

"He did, but Mom gave her a new arm," Sarah replied.

"Let me see," her sister insisted, reaching for the doll.

"No!" Sarah protested, pulling the doll closer. "You can't see!"

A struggle ensued as her sister tried to grab the doll. "That's my doll!" Penny screamed.

"You didn't ask me!" her sister retorted, pulling at the doll's arm.

"No!" Sarah cried again; her voice filled with terror.

As her sister tugged harder, the doll's arm snapped off once more, plunging Sarah into a state of panic.

THE SHINING PATH

"You're not asleep. This is a dream, but you're not dreaming," her uncle whispered. Suddenly, Sarah was somewhere else, without yesterday, today, or tomorrow.

She was three years old again, lying in her bed. An angel appeared and took her to heaven.

She saw Jesus and asked,

"Did I do good things? Do you watch me?"

Jesus smiled**, "Precious child, you I have chosen. Yes, I have always watched you, and I will continue to watch you"**.

"God, can I stay here forever and ever? This place is so beautiful and peaceful."

Sarah's voice was soft, filled with wonder. She looked up at the endless blue sky, dotted with fluffy clouds.

"You will, my child," a gentle voice whispered in her heart. It was comforting, like a warm hug on a chilly day.

"Can my mommy and daddy come too?" Sarah asked, her voice trembling slightly. She missed them terribly.

"Everyone you love will be here," the voice replied.

Sarah closed her eyes, imagining a place where everyone she cared about was happy and safe. "Will a big tree be in our backyard like the big one in my front yard?" **"And many more,"** the voice promised.

A sense of peace washed over Sarah. She felt loved and protected. "I love you, God," she whispered. As she opened her eyes, the world looked different. The colors were brighter, the air felt fresher. It was as if a piece of heaven had touched her heart.

"These are elders, can you count this many?"

Jesus asked, his eyes twinkling with amusement.

"Yes, I can count to ten!" Sarah replied confidently, her small fingers ready to count.

"Okay, you count ten, and I will count the other four and ten," Jesus said, smiling. As they counted together, a sense of peace washed over Sarah. It was as if the world stood still, and nothing else mattered.

"Do you know how much I love you?"

Jesus asked softly. Sarah's eyes widened with wonder. "Yes, I really know," she replied, her voice filled with certainty. "You died for my sins, but you're not dead because you're standin' right there!" Jesus chuckled, a sound like gentle rain. He lifted Sarah and placed her on a big, strong chair.

"**How do you know**?" he asked again, his voice full of curiosity. "Because I know a lot of important information, and you told me," Sarah said proudly. A small smile crept across her face. She felt a connection with Jesus, a strong bond that felt like a part of her. Sarah felt a surge of excitement and awe as Jesus spoke.

His words were like golden threads, weaving a tapestry of purpose in her heart.

"You know how much I love you," he said, his eyes filled with affection that touched her soul.

"There are three things you must do for me," he continued. Sarah nodded, her mind racing. She was ready.

"First, believe in the power in me. I will be with you always,"

Jesus said. Sarah's heart swelled with faith. She believed in him with all her might.

"Another, what I give to you, you will keep forever, and until," he said. Curiosity sparked in her eyes. What could this gift be? She was eager to discover it.

"Again, when you grow big you will write of what was, in a little book chosen. Will you do these things for me? Will you do these things for me?"

Jesus asked, his voice filled with anticipation.

Sarah replied, "Oh Yes, I will do these things for you!" Her heart pounded with a mixture of excitement and responsibility. She was ready to embark on this sacred journey. Sarah couldn't talk, but she could think. "I love you, Jesus!"

Sarah continuously remembers through her heart, mind, and soul. "I will do anything forever. I promise." She said. Jesus took her down from his big chair.

He put his hands on her head, and beautiful colors poured from her.

She held out her arms and twirled around and around. Magical twinkles of light followed her. "Oh, look at me, she said, " I am so beautiful!" **"Follow me,"** Jesus said. She followed and could see deep within the depths of her soul; her eyes took a picture.

THE HAUNTING

Sarah, who was four years old yesterday, was dreaming about the magical world of "The Wizard of Oz."

In her dream, a friendly angel appeared on the TV and invited her to join the movie. Excited and curious, Sarah agreed. Suddenly, she stood on a vibrant rainbow, soaring through the sky. The angel presented her with shimmering red slippers, explaining

that she could keep them forever.
Sarah was overjoyed and promised to
treasure them always.

Sarah's heart raced with excitement as
she held the shimmering red slippers in
her hands. The angel had promised
they were magical and could grant any
wish. However, a pang of guilt tugged
at her heart. She longed to share the
joy with her sister, who wasn't kind or
caring; but the slippers might make her
happier.

Despite the angel's assurances, Sarah
hesitated to put on the slippers. She
felt selfish for keeping such a wonderful
gift all to herself. But the angel
persisted, insisting that she try them

on. Reluctantly, Sarah slipped her feet into the shoes.

To her horror, the beautiful red slippers transformed into ugly, blue ones. Panic and confusion washed over her as she realized her mistake. The slippers were not the magical ones she had imagined, and she felt a pang of regret for her selfishness. Sarah was trapped in a terrifying nightmare world because of the ugly slippers. She couldn't escape and was surrounded by monstrous creatures and an evil witch. Fear and despair filled her as she realized she was lost in a dark and frightening place. A big purple monster flew around her. He had one large eye in the center of his head that was looking directly at her.

A big horn protruded from his forehead.

Sarah begged to go home, but the witch mocked her, saying her family didn't want her. Sarah cried and pleaded, desperately hoping for a way out. Sarah snapped her shoes together fast, thinking, "There's no place like home." She heard the evil witch laughing and saw monsters.

"Jesus, take me home!" Sarah screamed.

The witch squealed loudly, shaking Sarah's body.

"There is no Jesus! You filthy child. The promise you made was to me! I tricked you! Now I own you and you will live here forever!"

Sarah woke up from the terrifying nightmare, shaking and scared. The sweat was cold on her skin, and her heart pounded in her chest. She looked around the room, trying to shake off the lingering fear. The moonlight filtered through the window, eerie shadows on the walls.

She remembered the nightmare vividly. The evil witch, the monstrous creatures, and the endless darkness. It felt so real as if she had experienced it. Sarah shuddered, pulling the covers tighter around her. Her sister, Penny, stirred in her sleep.

"What's wrong with you, Sarah?" she asked sleepily.

"I had a bad dream," Sarah replied, her voice trembling. "A really bad dream."

Penny forcefully pulled the covers back over her head. "Too bad, there wasn't any monster there," she teased, "I was hoping he'd eat you up!"

Disappointed and terrified, Sarah also pulled the covers back over her head. She prayed to Jesus for protection, hoping the nightmare wouldn't return.

As soon as the words left her lips, sleep claimed her once more.

When she awoke, the world was bathed in soft morning light. A sense of peace washed over her as she realized she was floating high above the earth. Before her stood a radiant figure - Jesus.

"I give you my promise for being faithful and believing," he said, His voice gentle. Then, with a tender touch, He placed a helmet on her head and a breastplate on her chest. **"You will wear these until..."**

His voice trailed off, filled with a promise yet to be fulfilled.

"I also give you a spirit to forget yesterday, until..."

He continued....

His words carried a weight with a profound meaning.

"You believe in me, and I believe in you. The love you give me will reside within you, and I am with you also.

You follow with me, and I will follow with you also. You will not see me for a little while, but you will see me again. For I am in you, and you will be in me."

As the vision faded, Sarah found herself back in her bed, a sense of peace and courage filling her heart.

JOURNEY THROUGH THE SINGING GARDENS

"The truth is in the tree of life," she hears her uncle gently say to her as she travels again, to a place of yesterday, where tomorrow never comes, and today never was.

"Why did they put you in the river?" Sarah asked her sister.

Sarah was six years old today; her sister was eight. Her deep brown hair is all wet and she is wrapped in a towel.

"That's holy water, you have to be baptized if you want to go to heaven," she says.

"That water ain't holy water, it's the river," she said back to her. "I know it's the river, but they prayed, and they made the water holy. If you don't get into the river, you will see all the monsters in heaven. I won't see the monsters because I was washed clean," her sister says.

"Now, go away and stop bothering me!" she says.

Sarah sat on her bed and thought,

"My sister Penny was baptized today; she is pure and I'm not." She thought, and she felt dirty. Sarah started to cry.

"God, you know I always try to be

clean," She prayed. "I don't want to see the monsters in heaven. I want to be cleaned like my sister but, do I have to get in the water? Jesus, do you hear me? I love you and I know that you died for my sins." She cries and cries.

"Please don't show me the monsters in heaven." Then Sarah drifted off into her dreams. There is an angel with her. He was there and he said... "You can call me Michael. There are no monsters in heaven, and I will show you!"

The angel said softly, with a gentle smile on his face.

They float together on the softest pillow Sarah has ever felt. They were drifting higher and higher. They soon arrived at a beautiful castle in heaven, but it wasn't a castle; it was the biggest and most beautiful city that ever existed.

They walked up to the door, but it

wasn't a door; it was a gate. It had three gates, and the gates were like three pearls.

"Wow! Look at the pretty angels standing there," she tells Michael as Sarah points to the angels. Michael nods and replies,

"Those are the gatekeepers, welcoming us in."

Sarah's eyes widen in amazement as she takes in the grandeur of the heavenly city before them.

"Can you count them for me?" Michael asks. "One! Two! Three!" She counts out to him.

"Very good!" Michael says.
"I can even count to thirty, but

sometimes I get mixed up on fourteen and fifteen," she tells him.

"Sarah, did you like counting all the angels? Do not worry. There are not too many here to count. You will not be confused." Michael says in a gentle voice.

"Okay, but I already counted these three," Sarah says, as she points to the sky. "Those are just the beginning.

There is more waiting for you to count them," Michael replies, smiling at her enthusiasm.

Sarah and Michael continue to float through the heavenly city. They come across a vast library with books that glow with an inner light.

"Look, Michael!" Sarah says, pointing to a particularly large book. "Can we read that one?"

Michael smiles. "Of course, Sarah. Every book in this library holds knowledge of the universe. Choose any you like."

As Sarah reaches for the book, soft, ethereal music begins to play. The pages of the book seem to shimmer with images and stories. Sarah and Michael floated deeper into the heavenly city.

The buildings: if they could be called that, seemed to shimmer with a soft, iridescent light. They were more like living structures, changing, and adapting to the needs of their inhabitants.

"Look, Michael!" Sarah exclaimed, pointing to a magnificent garden. It was filled with flowers of every color imaginable, and their fragrance was intoxicating. But these were not ordinary flowers; they seemed to sing as they swayed in the gentle breeze.

"Hmm. Those are the Singing Gardens," Michael explained.

"Each flower's song is a different melody, and together they create a symphony of joy."

As they continued their journey, they came to a vast, crystalline river. Its waters were so clear that Sarah could see the bottom, where countless

rainbow-colored fish darted about.

 "This is the River of Life," Michael said.

"Its water brings eternal life and

healing to all who drink from it." Sarah

dipped her hand into the water and felt

a tingling sensation. It was as if the

water was infused with pure energy.

"It's so refreshing," she said, smiling.

They drifted on, passing through

bustling marketplaces filled with angels

trading goods that Sarah couldn't quite

understand. People were making pretty

things.

Other people were looking at big

books. "Everything here is perfect,"

Sarah whispered, her eyes wide with wonder. Michael nodded.

"And it will always be." As the sun began to set, casting the city in hues of pink and gold, Sarah felt a sense of peace she had never known before.

She looked at Michael, and in his eyes, she saw the love and kindness of a devoted friend.

"I love it here, Michael," she said softly. Michael smiled.

"And I love you being here, Sarah." Hold my hand, and I will show you."
She holds onto Michael's hand, and they take one step and Sarah counts,

"Four, five, six!" They take a step and Sarah counts,

"Seven, eight, nine!" They take another step, and Sarah counts,

"Ten, eleven, twelve! I can't count what's next," Sarah says to Michael. Her voice echoes slightly in embarrassment.

"That's because I told you, you will not be confused. We are back to where we started. So how many angels did you count?" Michael says, looking down at her. Like a proud father would.

"Twelve!" Sarah says to him.

"Then so it is!" He says with a bit of laughter behind his words.

"Wow!" she giggles, "Look at that house over there; it's so large and beautiful. You probably need to have a lot of money to have a house like that," Sarah remarks as she admires vibrant colors. "I wish my family could live in a house like that," she says. "I bet we would each have our own bedroom. It's so big, and look at all those colors," she adds.

"These are true colors," Michael says. "Would you like to go inside?" He asks.

"Should I take off my filthy shoes?" Sarah asks as she looks down at her dirty feet. "Can you crawl through the eye of a needle?" He asks. Why do you ask me a funny thing like that?" She replies.

"I choose to guide you," Michael says. "Do you understand what that means?"

"I sure do," Sarah replies, "I know a lot of important information."

They take a few more steps and Michael says, "Look! There are no monsters in here." Sarah looks around. Though the light is extraordinarily bright, it is not blinding, and she can still see.

"Wow! My mommy would really, really like these floors. "They are so shiny," Sarah exclaims, reaching down to touch the floor, it is so smooth and feels like glass. "At our house, my brothers drag me on a blanket to polish our floors. How do you get such a beautiful shine?"

She continues, her gaze turning to the walls, "And these walls, how did you make these pretty colors?" she inquires, admiring the richly painted surfaces. "Can I stay forever?"

Sarah asks Michael, looking up at him. "Yes, you can stay here forever and ever more, but not yet.

We are not ready for you yet. I will show you again when the time comes.

Believe what I say, and you will know the way." "Oh, that rhymes!"

She giggles and sings "Believe what I say, and you will know the way. Can I keep it? Can I sing it when I play hopscotch with my sister?" She asks.

They start to sing together and step as if they are playing hopscotch.

"Believe what I say," Jumping now with both feet and they sing. "And I will know the way" Sarah hears Michael giggle.

They hop on one foot in unison,

"And I will show you again, **Believe ...**"

They end their game of imaginary hopscotch, and Michael shows her a small cloud, about the size of a bed pillow.

"Look inside this cloud. What do you see?" He asks. "I see music," Sarah says back to him.

"You can see music? Michael asks, "What does music look like?" He giggles.

"Why do you ask me such a simple question? Look in there, you can see it too." She tells him.

"I know what I see. I was just wondering what your eyes may see. Being the eyes of a child, you may see things differently than I do."

"Oh well then! Do you see that sound right there?" Sarah points to the sound in the little cloud. Michael looks very closely, and he speaks.

"You mean that little chiming sound?"
"Yeah. That sound, you're so silly Michael, that's the only sound there is.

Of course, I mean the chiming sound."
She says to him.

"Okay. Yes, I see it" he says. "Well!
What does it look like?" She asks.

"Okay," Michael says to her. "We will
come back to this a little later.

There is more I want you to see," he
said, pointing to another small cloud.
"Look in this cloud and tell me what
you see."

Sarah peered intently into the
cloud form. "Ah, look!" she giggled
excitedly.

"What do you see?" Michael asks.

"Wow, look!" Sarah exclaimed; her
eyes wide with wonder. "I see a little

boy on top of the barn. He's all lit up with pretty lights!"

"The Rainbow Lights!" Michael replied excitedly. "They do glow!"

"Where did he get all those colors from?" Sarah wondered. "I think he's very happy. I bet I know what he's thinking. I bet he thinks he can fly."

"He is filled with the Holy Spirit," Michael said solemnly.

Sarah watched as the little boy in the cloud suddenly jumped and fell to the ground. She cried out, "Why doesn't he get up? Is he dead?" Suddenly, two angels appeared beside the boy, one at his head and one at his feet. Sarah's crying intensified.

"Why did the angels let him fall?" she sobbed.

"Why do you cry, child?" Michael asked gently. Look into the light." Sarah looked closely at the bright light.

Despite its intensity, she could still see. She focused harder and saw two angels standing near the little boy. Tears continued to stream down her face. Looking even closer, Sarah's eyes widened in amazement.

"Oh look!" she cried. "Two little white baby birds, as doves, pick up the boy and stand him on his feet!" Her tears stopped as she watched the scene unfold.

"You call him Bobby" ...Michael says...

"Bobby? My biggest brother in the entire world?" Sarah asks. Sarah remembered a story, her mother telling the kids about their brother.

She said that Bobby climbed onto the barn roof and fell off. He was hurt but he was okay.

"The river is like bread and wine," a voice said. One lives not without the other."

"Do you know who is talking to you?" Michael asked.

"Of course, I know it's Jesus, you silly Michael!"

Sarah replied with confidence.

"Do you know what he is saying to you?" Michael inquired further.

"Of course, I know," Sarah answered proudly. "I know important information because Jesus gave me bread with a book inside."

Sarah's uncle holds onto her hand. Thousands of souls chanted. Though they chant in many languages, they all chant the same thing. What they chant somehow is absorbed throughout every tiny element of Sarah's ever-existence. "Al---Le---Lu'---IA!" Very slowly they chant over and again. "Al---Le---Lu'---IA!" As they chant, Sarah notices that she is traveling.

She traveled yesterday, walking from tomorrow, and today was still to come.

She retained the feeling of traveling through a great telescope. Like a tunnel, it is long and dark. Like a bottle, it is wider at the bottom and narrower at the top.

She saw the amber light glowing precious and pure, far at the other end. She reached toward the light. She yearned to fill herself with the love that pours abundantly at the other end. She craved the light. Then instantly she noticed thousands of souls with her. reaching out into the souls, she was able to see-- and she heard. "Al---Le---Lu'---IA" Very slowly, in unison, they chanted repeatedly. Sarah felt the souls around her, each one with an eye that could see, feel, and hear. She sensed a profound connection to the souls that had been woven into the ancient tapestry. As her fingers traced their intricate patterns, she imagined hearing their stories, hopes, and fears."

Suddenly, a powerful scream erupted from her lips, echoing through the room. It was the voice of her own soul, a raw and intense cry that shook the very foundations of the tapestry.

"I know you!" she shouted, her words filled with a force that made the colors of the tapestry swirl and shift. The souls within the tapestry stirred, their energies surging and colliding. Sarah felt a surge of power, a connection to something greater than herself.

She knew, with absolute certainty, that she was not alone.

She touched the souls and heard and saw all things before and behind, and she knew each of them.

The voice of Sarah's soul screams, and every ear can hear!

"I know you!"   Sarah's uncle holds firm onto her hand, and he says, "Through adherence, I share my light, and you shall see."

Sarah saw music. She saw her family. Her whole family from all generations before and now.

The path is very wide. Thousands and thousands of souls are around her yearning to reach the light. They walk, and thousands of souls reach to embrace her, but can't stop. All craving the power in the light. with each step they take.

Sarah heard a cacophony of voices, speaking in strange languages simultaneously. They sounded confused as if babbling in unison, yearning for the same thing.

There were so many! Hebrew, German, Irish, French, Indian – and countless others. Sarah saw music, the music of all souls of her generation. Sarah staggered through the unforgiving desert. Her vision was hazy with thirst.

A faint rustling in the sand caught her attention, and she turned to see a mirage shimmering in the heat.

But as she approached, the mirage transformed into a lush oasis, an oasis of green amidst the endless sand.

A clear stream flowed through the oasis, surrounded by swaying palm trees.

As she drew closer, she heard a gentle voice calling her name.

Hope surged through her, a beacon in the darkness. The light, once distant, seemed to grow closer, promising relief and salvation. But the voices in her head grew louder, more insistent, pulling her in different directions.

Sarah began to stumble, her legs heavy with fatigue. The scorching sand burned her feet, and her thirst grew unbearable.

She was exhausted, but she refused to give up. Sarah felt a strong desire to reach the oasis, where she hoped to find light and a new beginning. The voices around her were loud and confusing, like many people talking at once in different languages. She wanted to reach the light very badly, but it was difficult because of the noise and confusion.

Sarah's body was tired and hurt from walking on the hot sand. She was also very thirsty. She felt like she couldn't walk any further and called out to God for help.

Her head was hurting, her feet were burning, and she did not have the strength to speak.

She did not even have the strength to breathe. "God, do you hear me? Please give me water, I'm so thirsty." Sarah thinks very loudly. Sarah pulls her hand from her uncle's grip to cover her ears, so she cannot hear.

She falls to the ground. She cannot walk anymore. So many different voices sound. Her uncle puts both his Hands-on her eyes when---

THE ETERNAL PATH

A harmonious symphony erupted from
the ones she could not yet see as
a chorus of languages blended in
perfect, celestial notes.

Sarah felt a surge of power as a wave
of pure, undivided love washed over
her, filling her to the brim.
Instantly and directly, as if given a
direct order, every language resounds
to sound, as a great and perfected

chime.

Lots of people stopped talking.

People were saying, "Hallelujah!"

Sarah saw her friends. They liked her.

She heard little bells.

Her uncle said, "This is real."

Sarah was happy. She felt small. She
felt as though she was home.

Sarah did not talk. She wrote what she
heard.

**"I that speak unto thee am He. Oh,
faithless generation, do you need a
sign?**

**Take up that household and follow
me. Ask what I shall give thee. Who
claims this divided generation? Are the
little ones divided? And when the little**

ones reach out for fulfillment, do you speak in parables they cannot understand? For you say tomorrow and tomorrow you say never comes. Now is the accepted time. The path to follow is narrow, why therefore do you take the wide?

Who claims this faithless generation?

"Now is the accepted time and every eye shall see."

Suddenly time traveled faster. The chiming sounds ring in total harmony at a distance. Soft humming sounds, a barely audible hum could be heard, the sound was coming from Sarah's soul like an amber light.

Sarah felt a magnetic pull as if her soul were being drawn into a blinding light. Overwhelmed by a sense of peace, she was catapulted into an extraordinary realm.

A breathtaking garden unfolded before her, a masterpiece of celestial design. Luminescent flowers, each a unique marvel, filled her vision.

Their petals seemed to shimmer with an inner light, casting iridescent hues across the ethereal landscape. A symphony of sound, a sweet and intoxicating melody, enveloped her.

A soft blue hue dominated the garden, creating a serene atmosphere. As Sarah reached to touch it, a gentle wind carried the sweet scent of the otherworldly blooms, revitalizing her senses. With every breath, she felt a surge of life, as if every cell in her body was being reborn.

Overwhelmed with a sense of belonging, Sarah knew she was home. Sarah felt a surge of power as if connected to the very essence of existence. A sense of limitless potential filled her, a realization of her ability to lead, to create, to simply be. The celestial music enveloped her completely, a wave of pure, unconditional love washing over her. Every particle of her being resonated with divine harmony. She could feel herself expanding, growing beyond her wildest dreams.

With a gasp of exhilaration, Sarah realized she could breathe freely, her spirit overflowing with joy. A sensation of weightlessness lifted her, and she soared through the celestial garden, a being of pure energy. In that moment, she knew herself completely, utterly, and profoundly.

A cocoon of translucent warmth enveloped Sarah, a comforting embrace as she ventured into the unknown. Gazing upward, she saw a crystalline star, its pure brilliance illuminating the ethereal landscape. A soft pastel blue washed over everything, a soothing canvas for the vibrant hues to come.

Lush apple trees laden with crimson fruit and a profusion of radiant flowers transformed the serene environment into an earthly paradise. Suddenly, her uncle materialized before her, a familiar yet otherworldly presence.

At his side, a mesmerizing interplay of colors unfolded: a deep blue, precious and pure, crowned by a golden halo.

As the blue shifted, the golden ringlet followed their connection, a testament to a profound cosmic law. With gentle hands, her uncle touched the translucent barrier surrounding her.

Curiosity ignited, Sarah looked beyond the cocoon and saw a vision of golden-brown hair, beneath which lay a sea of heavenly blue. The deeper she gazed, the more the blue intensified, revealing depths she couldn't fathom.

A longing to stay in this timeless moment consumed her. She wanted to exist forever within this realm of wonder.

Then, the blue permeated the cocoon, and a flood of sensations engulfed her.

"Do you know how much I love you?"

The words echoed in a relentless loop, a deep, soulful rhythm.

Sarah saw their faces - her children, her husband, her parents, her siblings, even her pets. Sarah saw music.

Each one is a canvas for this endless proclamation. It was a love that stretched beyond measure, back to a time before time, a love that consumed her.

Sarah was four. Standing in the kitchen doorway, she watched as her Mommy and Daddy talked. A sudden shift in their conversation caught her attention.

"The duck died," Daddy said, his voice heavy.

Mommy nodded; her eyes filled with sadness she couldn't understand.

"He swallowed a bee, and he died."

The world outside was a blur of panic. The turkey was a monstrous shadow chasing her, its gobble a deafening roar. The sharp crack of something against the ground and her father's angry shout provided a momentary distraction.

Sarah found Quacker in the pen, still and lifeless. His head felt cold in her small hands. She cried, a silent plea for understanding. "Do you know how much I love you, Quacker?" Daddy's words shattered the fragile world she was building.

"Sunday dinner," he said, his voice flat. The image of him carrying Quacker to that cold, concrete place was a nightmare she couldn't escape. Her mommy held her, promising we wouldn't eat him. But the fear was a seed planted deep within her.

Nightmares came in swarms, like angry bees. Sarah woke up drenched in sweat, heart pounding. She paced her room, a tiny prisoner of fear.

Then, a whisper, a promise: "Jesus help me! The bees are chasing me! Please save me!" Sarah prays. And at that moment, peace. A gentle hand, a soothing voice. "Hold out that leg," Daddy said, touching a balm to her stinging skin.

And then, a whisper, a promise:

"I work the works of him that sent me, even in your sleep."

Sarah opened her eyes, the world bathed in a new light. A path, a promise, a hope.

Sarah looked deeper and deeper into the blue and she saw

Sarah, just four years old, clung to her mother's leg, pleading, "Mommy, I don't want a shot!" Her mother reassured her, "It won't hurt," as they headed out the door. The long walk uptown to catch the bus was exhausting for the little girl. Sarah's eyes filled with tears as she grew more nervous.

When the bus arrived, the family boarded. The short ride to the nearest town was filled with Sarah's sobs. Even though her younger brother, Eddie, was only three, he tried to comfort her. He held her hand and said, "It'll only hurt for a little while, Sarah. Then it'll be over." After arriving at the health department, they sat on the chairs with other kids with teary faces. To Sarah, the wait was very stressful. Her little brother still held her hand as though to never let go. Eddie was just as scared as Sarah but was stronger because he was a boy. Eddie never showed fear of anything. He was never outwardly afraid of anything.

Then it happened. A woman just called our names. Eddie, Sarah, and her sister Kathy, who was five years old, started to walk to the room where the lady was calling. Her mommy was holding her baby brother Toby in her arms.

Kathy went first. Sarah gasped in fear as her older sister screamed, "No, you said it would only hurt for a second, and it hurt badly! Really, bad!"

"Oh no, Sarah screamed, "I don't want to get a shot. I don't want to get a shot." Sarah's mother handed her baby brother to a nurse and lifted Sarah to get her shot. Eddie had just received his shot. "Oh, Sarah, it didn't hurt. I just got mine. It only took a second. Don't worry." Her brave brother said.

The nurse gave baby Toby a shot, and he cried briefly before the nurse offered him a lollipop.

Sarah bit her thumb hard as the nurse poked her arm. "I don't want to get a shot," she shouted again.

"You already got the shot," her mother told her.

"I did? Oh, It didn't even hurt." Sarah exclaimed excitedly, taking the lollipop from the nurse.

As the time shifted, Sarah was once again back in Miss Emily's classroom. The room smelled of chalk and old wood. It was the day she learned about trees.

Miss Emily held up a tiny, green sapling. "This is yours to care for," she said, her voice firm. A little tree for each of them. She imagined it tall and strong, a home for birds, a place for picnics. Miss Emily talked about the sun, the soil, and the space a tree needed.

She listened, picturing her tree growing bigger and bigger. "Maybe I could build a treehouse! But what if my brother wanted to plant his tree nearby?"

Sarah raised her hand.

Miss Emily smiled. "That's fine, Sarah," she said.

"Trees like company." Sarah felt a thrill of excitement. Her little tree. Her responsibility. A piece of the world in her hands.

Her question hung in the air: "Can I take care of his tree too?" Miss Emily's answer was clear: "If he wants your help, that's fine. But the tree belongs to him." A sense of sharing and responsibility filled the room. They could share trees, but they were each on their own to nurture. No one wanted to give up their little green hope.

The first bell would signal their chance to choose their saplings. Excitement buzzed through the classroom. Suddenly, Sarah's uncle's hands were on her shoulders. "Write this down," he urged, his voice filled with a strange intensity.

She began to write, capturing the words as they tumbled out:

"What does this generation see? Are you lost? I promised clarity. Why don't you ask me? I will show you. Who owns this divided world? Are our

children broken? Is there no solid ground to stand upon? Does no one claim this lost generation? God is the supreme leader, and his plan is to be fulfilled. He called upon his chosen people to follow his guidance. This is his beloved son, listen to me! God desires a new way of life, free from the burdens of the past. He seeks those who will establish new foundations for the generation to grow. Those who embrace this new path must protect the innocence of the young and lead them toward a brighter future. To follow God's word, you must abandon the ways of this generation, and embrace a new, yet ancient way of life.

Those who resist this change will be left behind. God's chosen people will hear his voice and follow him.

United in purpose and strength. This generation lacks the strength and unity to build a new world. It is time for a new beginning, led by those who answer God's call.

So, how many did you count...?

As oneness thine eye be full.

Believe what I say, and you will know the way.

Those who believe will believe. Those who don't believe will believe." Sarah heard

"What do you see?" Sarah's uncle asks.

"Look into the light and you will see.

Through the light, you will hear." Sarah looked deep into the blue... And saw.

 "You're such a special little brother, you're my very bestest friend and I love you. We are going to buy our mom a new house. It is going to have real water, and we can drink the water." And she could hear,

"As oneness thine eye be full. This little one is my chosen one. He that has ears to hear, let him hear."

And she saw—She was many miles from any house. It is so hot.

She sees him knock at a door...

"Watch me, Daddy, watch me!

Are ya still watching me?"

She sees, "Draw your house like this..."

"You just glow in the dark."

And she heard,

 "As oneness thine eye be full...

You believe in me; I believe in you also.

The love you give me is within you and I am within you also.

You follow me. I will follow you also.

You will not see me for a little while, but then you will see me. I am with you, and I am with you always.

Fathers, take up thine household and follow me. Do the fathers know not the fathers? Do the sons know not the sons?

Do the mothers know not the mothers?

Do the daughters know not the daughters?

Does the family know not their family?

As the father knows me, even so, I know the father.

Are your doors locked?

Truly, I say unto you; I am the door, and I am the key.

You will not know at what time I will come.

Are you ready?   What do you see?

You ask what else I can give to you.

Now is the accepted time, and every eye shall see.

First, you take one step on one foot.

Pick up thine household and follow me.

Now you take one step on both feet.
Lay claim to that household and follow
me. Now is the accepted time. Lay
claim to this divided generation.

Follow me and I will guide you. You
follow with me; I follow with you too.

The father knows me, even so, I know
the father, for the father and I are as
one.

He that has ears to hear let him hear.
He that has eyes to see let him see.

Can you count them for me? Would
you like to count all of them?

You won't have to count so many that
you will be confused, every eye shall
see.

Over and over, it repeats...... Sarah traveled, to a place of until.

Sarah traveled to a place of no time yet has all the time to do everything forever and forevermore. A place where deep in the depths of her soul, her eye took a picture.

"What do you see?" Sarah's uncle asks. Her uncle is standing next to a tiny cloud. He puts one hand on the tiny form, and he holds the other out for her.

"What do you see?" Michael asks as he takes her hand.

Did you say you can see music? What does music look like? Look closely and you will see."

"You mean that little chiming sound?"
Sarah says to Michael as she looks
deeper into the little cloud. "Yes, I see
it."

"Well! What does it look like?" He
asked.

And she sees...

"Watch me, daddy, watch me. It is so
big and beautiful, and the colors are so
beautiful. I bet we could all have our
very own bedroom."

Sarah then hears her sister's
excitement.

"She's here! You are home!"

And her family's excitement.

"Come on, follow me, you'll see."

And she hears, "I wanna go!"

Then many visions appear again

"Where are you all going?"

"Follow me you will see."

"Do you need a sign or something?

It is a secret thing.

I know what you're getting for your

birthday."

"Let me give it to her."

Sarah saw Magical colors explode from

everywhere. The music roars yet is so

gentle. And she hears, "Look! She's

playing with her eyes closed." And she

saw, "No, she's not playing, she's

practicing

Do you hear what I hear?'

And she saw,

"She's not practicing! She's playing!

She's not practicing "**Do You Hear What I Hear**?"   She's playing,

"**I CAN'T HEAR**"

Sarah says "I can feel... I do not need to see to hear."

Each tiny note is a drop of pure color, one drop continues to follow the next in a perfect row of order, then blending to form a perfect melody in a clear, living-color reality.

Sarah saw the music as it fills everlasting true unconditional glorification into every tiny particle and element of her absolute existence.

 "Please can I stay here now? Please?"

Sarah's uncle holds firmly onto her hands and says, "Through adherence, I shine my light, and you will see. You cannot stay here now. We are not ready for you yet."

Michael puts his hands on one of the little enclosed forms. His hands penetrated right into the transparent covering that surrounded the little being. Sarah's uncle puts his hands on the little form and his hands penetrate the barrier.

Sarah put her hand on the little form and within an instant; she was there.

She saw amber. The beautiful color of amber was directly in front of her.

Beautiful amber lights surrounded her, and she knew that she belonged.

"I belong here, I came from here!" Sarah shouted out in her subconscious mind as the music of her soul surrounded her.

She could only gaze in total astonishment at what she saw.

"Look at all of these beautiful colors," Sarah thought to Michael, as she could only stare at all the beauty surrounding her.

"Would you like to go inside?" Her uncle asked, his hand gently touching hers as he enveloped her in a comforting, emerald-green shield of protection. Two large, emerald-green wings seemed to surround her, wrapping her snugly in a beautiful cocoon of security. "And every eye shall see," He giggles as they are instantly inside.   Sarah's heart was heavy as she remembered her uncle's words. She had felt so at peace in this beautiful place.

 "But why can't I stay here?" she asked, her voice trembling.

Her uncle sighed. "This is a place of transition, a place between life and what comes after. It's not meant to be a permanent home."

Sarah looked around at the shimmering room, the endless reflections of herself.

She felt a pang of sadness. "I don't want to leave," she said.

Her uncle knelt beside her. "I know, Sarah. It is hard to say goodbye to this world. But there's so much more waiting for you."

He took her hand and looked her in the eye. "Remember, you're not alone. I'll always be with you, watching over you." Sarah nodded, her eyes filling with tears. She knew her uncle was right, but that didn't make it any easier.

As they began to walk away, Sarah turned one last time to look at the room. She knew she'd never forget this place or the peace she felt here. But she also knew that her journey was far from over. As they stepped out of the room, Sarah found herself in the courtyard of a castle unlike any she had ever seen. Its walls were made of shimmering, translucent marble, and its towers reached high into the heavens.

The castle was surrounded by gardens filled with flowers of every color and scent imaginable. A gentle breeze carried the sweet fragrance of the flowers, and the air was filled with the sound of birdsong. Sarah felt a sense of peace and tranquility wash over her as she gazed at the castle. "This is your new home," her uncle said, smiling.

THE JOURNEY BEGINS

Sarah's eyes widened in amazement. She had never imagined a place so beautiful. As they walked towards the castle, she felt a sense of excitement and anticipation.

She knew that her journey had only just begun. "Look close," Her uncle says to her. Sarah looked to the side and saw her daddy. He was walking down a long golden staircase in the center of the room. And in his hands, he holds something. "What do you see?" Sarah's uncle asks. "Look into the light, look closely and you will see it," Michael says.

Sarah looked into the light. It was very bright, but she could still see.

"Oh, I see it!" she giggled as she looked closer into the beautiful, soft blue light surrounding her daddy.

"What is it that you see? "Michael

"Oh, my wings!" Sarah says.

Sarah saw her beloved wings.

"Quacker! Oh, Quacker... Oh, how I missed you."

Sarah says to her duck.

Sarah giggled as she watched her daddy take each step closer to her.

"Do you know how much I love you?" He says as he tenderly hands Sarah her duck.

"Oh, no! ... I can't ever forget... I will never forget..."

"Would you like to go upstairs? I will show you each step, one step at a time,"

Sarah's daddy says as they take one step and another. The light was very bright, but she could still see.

She watches herself glide ever so gently. She glides through the air, as though it were a movie playing in slow motion. She continued to envision herself soaring through boundaries as if teleporting to a place beyond the realm of the ordinary.

Sarah saw golden hair that shimmered in the sunlight as he galloped past. 'He's incredibly gentle,' her friend exclaimed, her voice filled with admiration.

'See, he's so gentle. Get on him."

"I've never ridden a horse before. Are you sure he will like me? What if he throws me over the fence?"

"He won't throw you, touch him, he's very gentle. Put your foot in here and throw your leg over the top. Just hold on tight and you won't fall off. Now, listen, when you want to slow down, pull slightly on these reins and he will slow down. When you want to stop, pull harder and say, 'Whoa whoa,' and he will stop. Okay, are you ready?"

"Wait! I don't know if I'm ready. What if...?" "Giddy-up." "Look! I'm riding him! I'm riding!

Do you see me!? Are you watching me? I'm riding him!"

Sarah joyfully shouts as she glides without her feet ever touching the ground.

"Where are you?" Sarah thought, looking around the vast, open pasture. She didn't see her friend anywhere.

Suddenly, everything seemed to move faster. The horse she was riding was galloping at an alarming pace. She pulled the reins, but it wouldn't slow down.

She pulled harder and harder but to no avail. "Oh no!" She thought, panic rising.

"Jesus, help me! Please help me! I'm going to crash!"

Sarah looked up and saw the fence getting closer. The horse raced faster, and she pulled the reins with all her might.

"Open the gate!" She screamed. "Mary! Open the gate!"

Sarah fell to the ground, unable to speak. As she tumbled and spun, magical droplets of color surrounded her. A loud humming sound filled her ears, and strange voices echoed from a distance. Sarah felt confused and disoriented.

"God, can you hear me?" She cried. "Where am I?

These voices... where are they coming from?"

Sarah looked up and saw a figure glowing like a pearl. "Are you, my angel?" She whispered, her words drifting softly through the air.

Sarah lay motionless on the ground, feeling numb and shocked. Suddenly, they were right beside her.

"Hurry! Please hurry!" Sarah's friend cried. "He threw her off! He ran right up to the gate and threw her off. The gate wasn't even closed! She thinks I'm an angel. Do you think she will be okay?"

Sarah's eyes were wet, and her shoulders shook with sobs. Her father's voice, filled with concern, echoed in her ears.

 "It's all right, Sarah, don't cry," he repeated, his hand gently stroking her hair.

"Are you alright? Look at me, are you alright?"

She tried to nod, but it was difficult. Her father's worried gaze met hers, and she felt a surge of comfort. His presence was a warm blanket, shielding her from the cold, dark storm raging inside.

Sarah looked up and saw twelve rooms, each painted a distinct color.

"Each room has a door, and the door was like a gate." Sarah's father said.

"The gate can never be shut," and...

"The gate will never be shut," Michael

added.

Each gate was like one pearl, and at every third pearl, there was one angel.

One angel stood outside of every third room.

As Sarah listened to the faint little chime sounds that seemed to be coming from every room, she asked her father, "Where are those chimes coming from?"

It sounded like each room had a unique sound. "Don't let the colors bleed," Michael said as he walked closer to the rooms having unusual colors and sounds.

"I will show you," he said. "Believe what I say, and you will know the way." Sarah's father held onto her hand, and they took one step.

They were now standing at a door. On each side of the door was a pole, and each pole was carved like one tall, gigantic angel.

"Look, I want you to see," he said as he reached into his pocket and pulled out an angel.

"I carved these little ones in my workshop." Her father held out his hand for her to see. She looked into his hand and saw a little white angel, just for her.

Sarah was sitting at the lunch table with her fourth-grade class. She took something off the lunch tray.

Sarah held it tight... she was getting off the school bus and crossing the street.

She walked up the sidewalk. And into the house.

Sarah's daddy was holding her little brother on his knee. Sarah holds it tighter and tighter while waiting to sit on her daddy's lap... Her brother is finished showing his school papers... Sarah climbed up on her father's lap. "I have something for you," she said. "I've been holding onto it all day." "What do you have for me?"

her father asked. Sarah opened her hand for her father to see the olive she had taken from the lunch tray. Her father opened his hand, and Sarah gave him the olive. He was incredibly happy.

Sarah turned toward the door. Her
sister was waiting at the door, ready to
sit on her father's lap, and in her hands,

she held something. They both looked
to see all the olives in their father's
hand. Sarah took one step and could
hear heavenly musical sounds gently
flowing from every room as they
passed. Her father held onto her hand,
and they entered a room. "This is your

room, Sarah." Her father said as he showed her, her very own room. The walls were a kaleidoscope of color, each hue blending seamlessly into the next like a masterpiece painted by a celestial artist. The effect was that of a living wallpaper, pulsating with vibrant energy.

The room felt alive as if the colors themselves were breathing and dancing.

The ceiling was a breathtaking spectacle, a series of towering domes adorned with intricate paintings of angels and heavenly spirits. Their ethereal forms seemed to float across the canvas, their wings shimmering with iridescent hues. The light from a hidden source washed over the paintings, casting long, dancing shadows that added to the mystical atmosphere. Emerald, green was the dominant color, a breathtaking hue that swirled and danced among the other pastels.

The room was filled with a gentle hum, a soft melody played. Like a trumpet, it blew very low... A trumpet hummed throughout the room.

"What is that sound?" She whispers. "Why am I whispering?" She whispers again.

"This is a secret place, and this is a secret thing." Her daddy whispers back.

Her daddy holds onto her hand as many figures surround them.

Instantly, they are of human form, and just as they were human, they were not.   There are other people with her. Many people surround Sarah. "What do you see?

Can you see music?

Did you ever see floors that shine like this?" Her daddy asks.

Suddenly, Sarah doesn't need to see to hear great power as it embeds into every tiny particle of her ever being.

Sarah reaches out, into the souls, into the chimes, and feels a tremendous overfilling power of pure undivided love, and the only thing she could think of was love. I want to stay here forever! Sarah says as she takes one step and hears...

"You cannot stay here now; your time has not yet come."

They took one step and another, and her daddy took her hand, and they walked up a walkway made of gold.

On the side of the walkway was a tree.

"Do you see the limbs on this tree?" Sarah's daddy asks as he points to the tree.

"Do you see the limbs on this tree?" Repeatedly and again, it repeats.

Sarah continued to travel, travelling to a place long forgotten. Somewhere

where she remembered something,
and deep into the depths of her soul,
her eyes took a picture...

Sarah's father sings a lollypop song.

Lollipop, Lollipop

Oh, Lolli-Lolli-Lolli

Lollipop, Lollipop

Where's the little lollipops?

"I chose it just for you." Who picked
the lollipop?

"Oh, I hear them!" Sarah shouts. I see
them!"

"What color is it for me!?" Sarah asks.

"Lollipop!"---Amber and it is you!"

Who has seen the Lollipops?

Her daddy sings

Time,"--- "Amber Repeatedly, it

repeats

"Look, do you see 'me? Do you see it?

It was lost in time." "My school

papers!" Sarah shouts.

"Look at the eyes, do you see EM?"

"Where did you find EM?" She asks.

"Look in the mirror. See 'EM?   And do you see it?"

"Let me show you!"

"I found 'EM lost in time."

"What? Do your eyes see? .... Time? Oh, then look at it.

Look at EM. Now turn it around and look at ME?"

"What do your eyes see? What do your ears hear?

You do see what I see."

"This time, you can show it to your mother. Tell her where you found EM."

And she saw, and she heard...

I now give forth to you, time. All Time. Yesterday, Today, Forever, and Always."

Time then, and time again.

"And I am... And in my hands, I hold something."

And She heard...

"Come. Come. Come to me. And I will show you!"

An angelic voice sang softly as she traveled. She traveled to a place where a second spanned an eternity. "Time then and Time again." A place deep in the depths of her soul, her eyes took a picture.

On the bedside table, the clock was still at **1:00 AM**.

What do you see?

For you, Little Star,

Tobuscus.

"Nine months after conception, on my birthday, a miracle unfolded. My son emerged from the cosmic womb still inside a celestial bubble bathed in starlight and was born.

The melody she remembered again was...

When you wish upon a dream, a hope, a wish, a golden gleam. The heart's desire, a shining star, a wish fulfilled, not distant far.

A twinkling hope, a magic sight, A dream come true, a pure delight."

"Do you see music? What does the music look like?"

A newborn's cry, a hopeful sound, A family's joy, forever bound. A tiny soul, a precious sight, A future's promise, pure and bright. But fate can change, a tragic turn, A heart may break, a spirit yearns. A silent note, a missed refrain, A family's sorrow, endless pain. A heavenly choir, a distant call, Awaiting loved ones, one and all.

His arrival illuminated the delivery room, a new soul entering the world."

A radiant being...My Son- My little star,

Made in the USA
Las Vegas, NV
11 November 2024

11532689R10135